DATE DUE			

Weather Watchers

Sunshine

Cassie Mayer

Heinemann Library
Chicago, Illinois

Photo research by Tracy Cummins, Tracey Engel, and Ruth Blair
Designed by Jo Hinton-Malivoire
Printed and bound in China by South China Printing Company

10 09 08 07 06
10 9 8 7 6 5 4 3 2 1

Library of Congress Cataloging-in-Publication Data
Mayer, Cassie.
 Sunshine / Cassie Mayer.-- 1st ed.
   p. cm. -- (Weather watchers)
 Includes bibliographical references and index.
 ISBN-13: 978-1-4034-8410-9 (library binding-hardcover : alk. paper)
 ISBN-10: 1-4034-8410-4 (library binding-hardcover : alk. paper)
 ISBN-13: 978-1-4034-8418-5 (pbk. : alk. paper)
 ISBN 1-4034-8418-X (pbk. : alk. paper)
 1. Sunshine--Juvenile literature. I. Title. II. Series.
 QC911.2.M39 2007
 551.5'271--dc22
                              2006007906

Acknowledgments
The author and publisher are grateful to the following for permission to reproduce copyright material:
Corbis pp. **4** (cloud; rain, Anthony Redpath), **5** (G. Schuster/zefa), **7** (Royalty Free), **8** (Theo Allofs), **9** (zefa/Sergio Pitamitz), **10** (Chris Sattlberger), **11** (Royalty Free), **12** (Royalty Free), **13** (Galen Rowell), **14** (Reuters), **15** (epa/Karl-Josef Hildenbrand), **16** (Richard Klune), **17** (zefa/S. Andreas), **18** (Royalty Free), **19** (zefa/Jason Horowitz), **20** (George D. Lepp), **21** (ROB & SAS), **23** (heat wave, Reuters; snow scene, epa/Karl-Josef Hildenbrand); Getty Images pp. **4** (lightning; snow, Marc Wilson Photography), **6** (Tim McGuire).

Cover photograph reproduced with permission of Corbis (Howard Kingsnorth/zefa).
Back cover photograph reproduced with permission of Corbis (George D. Lepp).

Every effort has been made to contact copyright holders of any material reproduced in this book.
Any omissions will be rectified in subsequent printings if notice is given to the publisher.

Contents

What Is Weather?

Weather is what the air is like outside.
Weather can change all the time.

A sunny day is a type of weather.

What Is Sunshine?

Sunshine is light from the Sun.

Sunshine feels warm
on your skin.

Sunshine heats the land.

Sunshine heats the oceans.

The Sun rises in the morning.
Then it is light outside.

The Sun sets in the evening.
Then it is dark outside.

Sometimes the Sun is high.
Sunshine is strong when the Sun is high.

Sometimes the Sun is low.
Sunshine is weak when the Sun is low.

Sunshine and the Seasons

Sunshine is strong in the summer.
Summer days can be hot.

Sunshine is weak in the winter.
Winter days can be cold.

Sunshine Around the World

Some places have strong sunshine.
These places are warm all year.

Some places have weak sunshine.
These places are cold all year.

Sunshine Safety

Sunshine can hurt your skin.
Always stay covered in the Sun.

Sunshine can hurt your eyes.
Never look right at the Sun.

How Does Sunshine Help Us?

Living things need sunshine to grow.

Sunshine is an important part of our weather. Sunshine is also fun!

What to Wear in the Sun

hat

sunglasses

sunblock

long-sleeve shirt

Picture Glossary

summer the time of year when it is the warmest

winter the time of year when it is the coldest

Index

Note to Parents and Teachers

This series introduces children to the concept of weather and its importance in our lives. Discuss with children the types of weather that they are already familiar with, and point out how weather changes season by season.

In this book, children explore sunshine. The photographs were selected to engage children while supporting the concepts presented in the book. The text has been chosen with the advice of a literacy expert to enable beginning readers success reading independently or with moderate support. An expert in the field of meteorology was consulted to ensure accurate content. You can support children's nonfiction literacy skills by helping them use the table of contents, headings, picture glossary, and index.